Historic Military Press

The Pas de Calais, Spring 1940. A member of ground crew helps a pilot from the 5th Staffel, JG27, through his pre flight checks. Soon after the aircraft would join the massed ranks of Messerschmitt Bf109s in making another sortie over the English countryside.

ALEXANDER NICOLL

To find out about other titles produced by
Historic Military Press visit our website at www.historicmilitarypress.com.
Alternatively please write to us free of charge at
Customer Services, Historic Military Press,
Freepost SEA 11014, Pulborough, West Sussex, RH20 4BR,
or telephone our freephone number: 0800 071 7419.

HISTORIC MILITARY PRESS

GERMAN FIGHTERS
OVER THE UNITED KINGDOM 1939-45

© Copyright Alexander Nicoll, 2001.

First published 2001 by Historic Military Press,

ISBN 1-901313-07-7

Writing a book of this nature has required much in-depth research into the various types and designs which are covered. To this end mention must be made to the following authors (and their books) for having had the foresight to write these excellent reference guides. 'Dowding and the Battle of Britain', R. Wright, Corgi, London, 1979. 'Fighter - the story of the Battle of Britain', L. Deighton, BCA, London, 1978. 'The Hardest Day', A. Price, Macdonald, London, 1979. 'Spitfire Summer', P. Haining, Selecta Books, Devizes, 1995. 'Sussex Airfields in the Second World War', R.J. Brooks, Countryside Books, Newbury, 1993. 'The Chanctonbury Crashes', Martin Mace, Historic Military Press, Storrington, 1998. 'Men of the Battle of Britain', Kenneth G. Wynn, CCB Associates, South Croydon, 1999. 'Fighters and Bombers of World War II', Kenneth Munson, Peerage Books, London, 1983. 'The Battle of Britain', Richard T. Bickers, Doubleday, Toronto, 1990. 'The Battle of Britain, Then and Now', Winston G. Ramsey (ed), After the Battle, London, 2000. 'Battle over Sussex', P. Burgess & A. Saunders, Middleton Press, Midhurst, 1990. 'Blitz over Sussex', P. Burgess & A. Saunders, Middleton Press, Midhurst, 1994. 'Bombers over Sussex', P. Burgess & A. Saunders, Middleton Press, Midhurst, 1995.

The author and publishers are deeply indebted to the following people. Unless indicated, all the photographs and relics shown in this book come from one amazing private collection. We are also grateful to the Royal Air Force Museum at Hendon, for the allowing us to reproduce the photographs on pages 3, 24 and 28; the West Sussex Record Office for the map on page 16; the Historic Military Press Collection; Mr. Geoff Goatcher for allowing us to use his sketches; and Mr. A. Oliver for the use of the pictures on pages 29 and 32.

Printed in the United Kingdom by
Selsey Press Ltd., 84 High Street, Selsey, Chichester, PO20 0QH
Telephone: 01243 605234

HISTORIC MILITARY PRESS
Green Arbor, Rectory Road, Storrington, West Sussex, RH20 4EF. Telephone/Fax: 01903 741941

www.historicmilitarypress.com.

Very occasionally a German aircraft would have come to be on British soil by choice. Perhaps the most famous German aircraft crash, which made headline news around the world, is that relating to the arrival of Rudolph Hess.

Hess held the second most senior post in wartime Germany, that of Deputy Fuehrer of the Third Reich. After the outbreak of the Second World War, and without the knowledge of Hitler, Hess set about trying to broker a peace agreement between the Germans and British. It was a tragedy, he believed, for Germans and British, "Aryan blood brothers", to fight one another in war. Despite being forbidden to fly by Hitler, Hess managed to persuade Messerchmitt to allow him to undertake long distance training flights over Germany. On the 10th May 1941 he took off from Augsberg, dressed as a flight lieutenant in the Luftwaffe, on one of these flights. However, the course he had scribbled in pencil on his map suggested that this was to be a training flight with a difference.

Several hours later, at about 11pm, his plane crashed to earth at Bonnyton Farm, near Eaglesham in Scotland. Hess had been trying to reach the estate of the Duke of Hamilton, with whom Hess believed he would be able to discuss his peace plan. Unable to find an exact place to land and with his aircraft starting to stall, he bailed out and floated down on a Scottish farm. Unarmed he allowed himself to be captured by a local farmwoker who pointedly informed Hess that he would happily make use of his pitchfork should Hess 'try anything funny'. Suffering from a broken ankle Hess was first taken to a Glasgow hospital, before finally ending up in the Tower of London. Here Churchill ordered that he be treated with dignity, whilst from Germany came anguished cries of disbelief and disavowal. Hitler ordered that the world be informed that he [Hess] had taken leave of his senses. Hess had made the flight in a Messerschmitt Bf110 that carried the serial number 3869. Shown here is a part of that aircraft, that can now be seen in the RAF Museum at Hendon. Still visible on this piece of panel work is part of the original German markings.

(By kind permission of the RAF Museum Hendon)

As for the remainder of the wreckage, some of the fuselage and engines have survived, with the former lying at the Imperial War Museum at Duxford. One of the two engines can also be found in the collection of the RAF Museum. Many smaller items can be found in private collections, such as the oxygen mask that Hess had been wearing in the moments before he abandoned his aircraft. The farm worker who welcomed Hess on landing was David McLean. In 1954 he was asked if he had any pieces left from the crash, to which McLean replied 'only one - his oxygen mask'. Now in a private collection, McLean recalls he found this relic some days later, in a field over which Hess passed. Despite his actions and alleged peaceful intentions, Hess was still an ardent supporter of the Nazi party and its regime. Subsequently, in 1946, he stood before the Nuremberg war crimes tribunal. He was sentenced to life imprisonment, a term he served to the end in solitary confinement at Spandau Prison in Berlin.

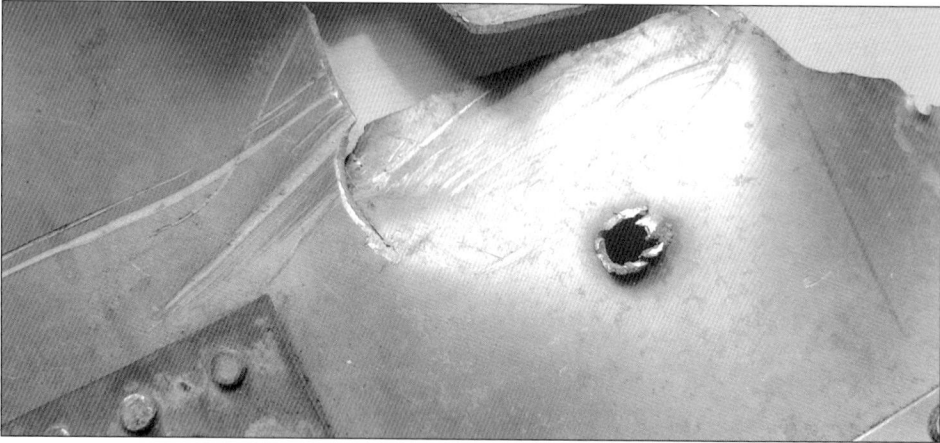

Above. For many years now the debate over aircraft archeology has raged fiercely. What is beyond dispute is the fact that, in a great many cases, the recovery of parts from a stricken aircraft, whatever its nationality, often provides us with clues as to what might have taken place in the moments prior to the crash. The piece of tailplane shown here is just such a relic. The Battle of Britain was just 6 days from its end when, on the 25th October 1940, the Luftwaffe carried out freelance fighter sweeps over the south coast. Soon after being intercepted by RAF fighters a Messerschmitt Bf109E-1 fell to ground at Lidham Hall Farm, Guestling, East Sussex. Once cleaned this fragment almost certainly shows the reason why this German fighter crashed. The hole almost in the centre is distinctive of those produced by the passing of a .303 bullet - the characteristic 'lip' is clearly evident. This suggests that the Bf109 was a victim of the intercepting RAF Squadrons. All of the RAFs front-line fighters during the Battle of Britain were armed with .303 machine guns. The Hurricane had eight, whilst the Spitfire four. The 'lip' is most important, as it helps the archaeologist establish that the hole was indeed produced by a bullet, as opposed to one that may have been the result of a rivet being torn out, or the surface being punctured by another object in the crash.

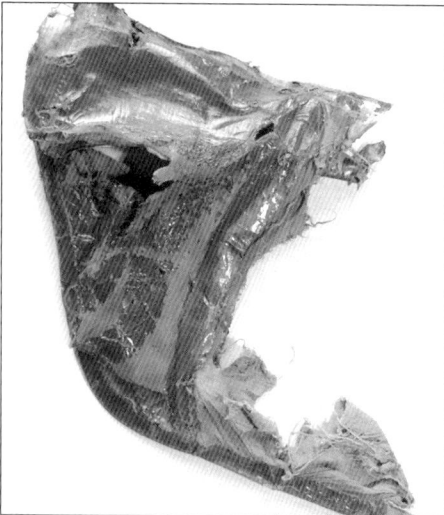

Left. Staying with the Lidham Hall crash site, this larger piece is in fact part of the aircraft's tailplane. The information to be gleaned from this piece is different, and does not relate to the reasons for the crash. Instead, an enthusiast can learn details of the colours used by the Luftwaffe during the camouflaging of this particular Bf109. Despite having been buried for over 50 years the fabric covering the metal framework is remarkably well preserved. The upper surface was the standard dark olive green, and the underneath the equally common sky blue. What wasn't normal is the shine that the fabric now carries. This is the result of the preservation treatment that this relic had to undergo. As soon as any surviving fabric is exposed to the air, decay very quickly sets in. One of the most common methods of preservation is to cover the material with a varnish.

Two identification plates from the Battle of Britain. Both are from Bf110s, a simple deduction if you look at the bottom stamped number. In both the identifying number, '110', is present. The top plate comes from a Messerschmitt Bf110D that crashed at Crowhurst, Surrey on the 6th September. The second example is from a Bf110C that fell to earth on the 7th October, this time at Kingston Dairy Farm, Long Bredy, Dorset.

Left. Aviation archaeology is not without its dangers. Almost without exception a site under excavation is likely to contain, at the very least, unexploded ammunition and, in the worse case scenarios, unexploded bombs. This link of four remarkably well preserved machine gun bullets is a perfect example. Following fighter combat over Elham, Kent, on the 5th September 1940, a Messerschmitt Bf109E-1 crashed near Appledore Station. The pilot, Lt. Strobel, was killed. It was a warm and sunny day in 1986 that the remains of the aircraft were uncovered.

What made the day all the more remarkable was the fact that it turned out to be the anniversary of the pilot's birthday. Strobel had been born on the 5th September 1915!

Despite some crash damage, all the details on these rounds can still be clearly seen - right down to the letter 'Z' embossed on each of the four links.

Top right. This group of excavated rounds originates from another Bf109 crash site, though this time in East Sussex. This German fighter was shot down by a No. 605 Squadron Hurricane flown by Flight Lieutenant McKellar. The date was Monday the 7th October 1940, and the crash site at Mayfield Flats, Hadlow Down near Heathfield.

These bullets are obviously in a worse condition than the previous examples, with some having apparently fired off. This may have occurred in the impact, or during the extreme temperatures generated by the fire that consumed the aircraft immediately after the crash. Worthy of note is the fact that these bullet cases are all dated 1938.

This bit of archaeology therefore provides a small piece of evidence to the fact that the German High Command, mindful of the fact that war in Europe would not be long in coming, had been manufacturing and stockpiling military supplies in large quantities in the years leading upto 1939.

Bottom right. In even poorer condition are these bullets salvaged from the crash site of a Bf110 at The Droke, Upper Waltham in East Sussex.

These show the classic sign of bullets that exploded during the crash. In some cases the heads have remained in place despite the gunpowder in the casing having exploded, helping produce some of the characteristic rupturing on three of these rounds.

Throughout the war years, and in the Battle of Britain in particular, the British countryside echoed to the sound of exploding ammunition following a plane crash. Mr. C. Turner, a farmer from Washington in West Sussex, describes this common phenomenon:

"The plane, a Messerschmitt Bf110, crashed at Church Farm, Rowdell, near Washington, on the 4th September 1940. The impact was so severe that the plane buried itself to a depth of some 15ft. The whole area was dangerous as bullets in the crater kept going off. Occasionally you could even hear the whistle of a passing bullet. Needless to say this kept the spectators at bay!"

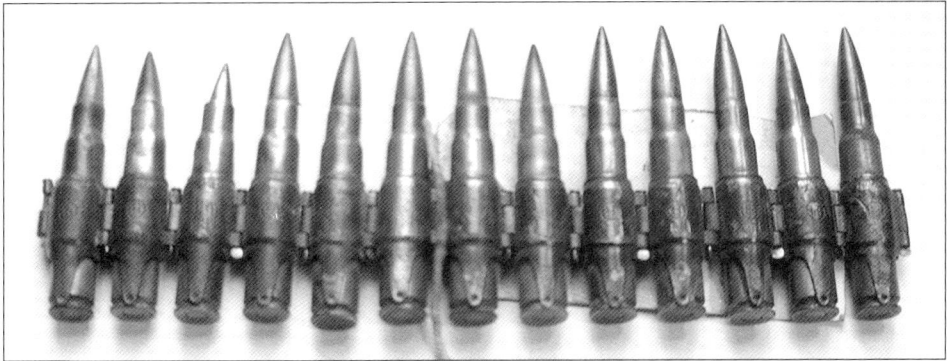

Above. A total of 13 bullets remain on this impressive section of an ammunition belt recovered from the Bf109 crash site at Lidham Hall Farm. The Messerschmitt Bf109 carried (in the earlier variants) a formidable array of weapons. There were two 7.92mm Rheinmetall-Borsig MG-17 machine guns mounted above the engine, and two 20mm cannons mounted one in each wing. Each machine gun had a supply of 1,000 belted rounds, whilst the cannon 500 rounds stored in a drum. This may sound impressive, but depressing the firing button for a few seconds too many could see the pilots entire magazine disappear!

Below. No excavation seems ever complete without the presence of the ubiquitous mechanical digger! This 'dig' at Knightswood, North Baddersley, Hampshire proved to be no different. The full story, however, started back in the early days of the Battle of Britain. On the 13th August 1940 air activity was fierce, for this was the day that Goering had set for 'Aldertag'. Bad weather meant zero hour was postponed until 2pm, after which the skies over southern England became full of aircraft. In the confusion of scattered aerial battles the RAF lost 13 aircraft, whilst the Luftwaffe some 34. One particular Messerschmitt Bf110C-4, from 1/ZG2 had been allocated to a fighter escort force that soon ended up in the skies over the south of England. Above Winchester they were intercepted and this aircraft, crewed by Uffz. Labusch and Lt. Munchmeyer, was shot down. Munchmeyer was able to bale out, though badly wounded, and was captured. The pilot, Labusch, was killed. The aircraft crashed into open farmland, burst into flames and subsequently burnt out.

Right. Shown here is a relatively unique souvenir from the air war over the United Kingdom during the Second World War. This superb model of a Bf109 was only crafted in recent years, but appears here by virtue of the metal from which it was cast. On the 29th August 1940, a Bf109 was shot down during combat and crashed at New Lodge Farm, Hooe, in East Sussex. The pilot, Oblt. Wipper had bailed out only to subsequently die from his wounds. In 1973 the site was excavated and a range of parts recovered. Amongst these were the first aid kit, the propeller boss and blade and a large number of fragments from the Daimler-Benz engine. Some of these unrecognisable lumps of engine alloy were smelted down and re-cast into the shape we see here.

Below. On the 23rd April 1994 an excavation team visited Knightswood. This was not the first such operation, for an earlier 'dig' had already uncovered a number of pieces of the aircraft including an engine. On a pleasantly cool day the site of the

original excavation was reopened. A fair quantity of wreckage was found, some of which had obviously been thrown back by the earlier 'dig'. A second indent in the field was then examined and very quickly it became evident that this area had never been touched. Indeed judging by some of the items found it also seemed likely that the wartime recovery crews had also paid scant attention to this part of the field. As this second hole, excavated by the mechanical digger, reached a depth of 15ft, the finds began to pour in. One of the first was this part of a fuel tank strap **(bottom)**. The fuel tanks for the Bf110, located in the wings between the engine nacelle and the fuselage, were held in place by a number of webbing straps. On the end of each strap, as shown here, is a bolt that attaches the strap to the mainframe.

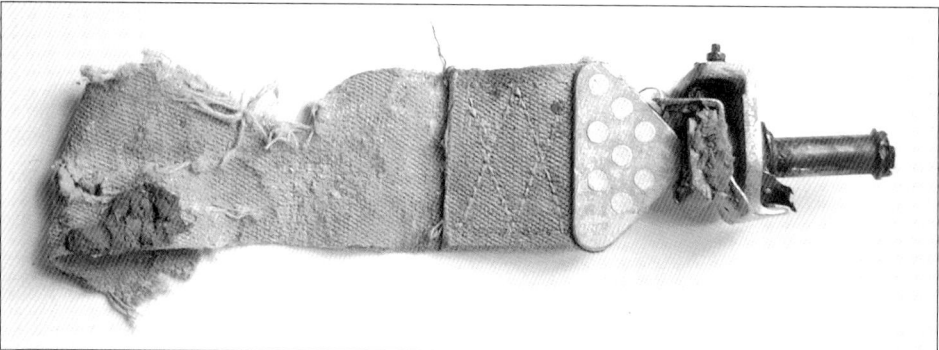

Right. As the dig progressed the number of recognisable fragments found continued to grow. In the foreground of this photograph is an undercarriage leg and, just behind it, a complete rubber tyre. Both were found to be remarkably well preserved, especially so when you consider the time that they had been buried. Other major parts that also saw daylight once more were three propeller blades, the remaining engine (the other being recovered in the previous excavation) and a whole host of other airframe parts. The latter were all gathered together and taken away in the hope of finding the aircraft number during cleaning. Nothing from the cockpit was found, though large amounts of ammunition were present.

Right. Local police and Home Guard can only watch as the remains of the North Baddersley Bf110 still smoulder. No one can be sure how much time had past since the crash before this photograph was taken, but contemporary records show that in many cases a crash site could burn for many days after. Pictures such as these are vital to the aviation archeologist. Not only do they suggest what may be found at a site but more importantly they provide an exact location. Compare this photograph to the earlier one with the mechanical digger and it is apparent that it is the same location.

Below. In almost every major excavation one or more of the parts recovered will also help provide clues as to the identity of the victim. Such details will help support contemporary wartime records. It was a warm and sunny day in 1984 when a JCB was used to excavate the site of a Messerschmitt Bf109E that crashed into a field at Blackwall Marsh, Methersham near Rye. Digging started about 400 yards southwest of Merthersham Bridge, and by the time work stopped at 4pm a wide selection of fragments had been uncovered. These included the propeller hub; a third of the Daimler-Benz engine block; part of the stick; compass; several plates, and even a large piece of the tail canvas.

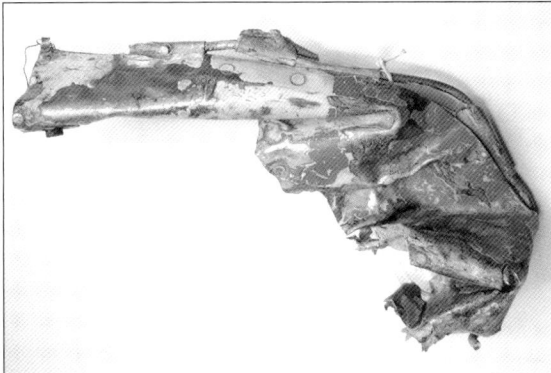

From the piece of wreckage shown here the unit was identified - JG 53. The JG, or Jagdverbaende, were fighter units equipped by the Bf109. The JG 53 had a unique marking for their aircraft - a red band painted round the nose of the Bf109. It is part of this red band that is evident on this fragment of engine cowling.

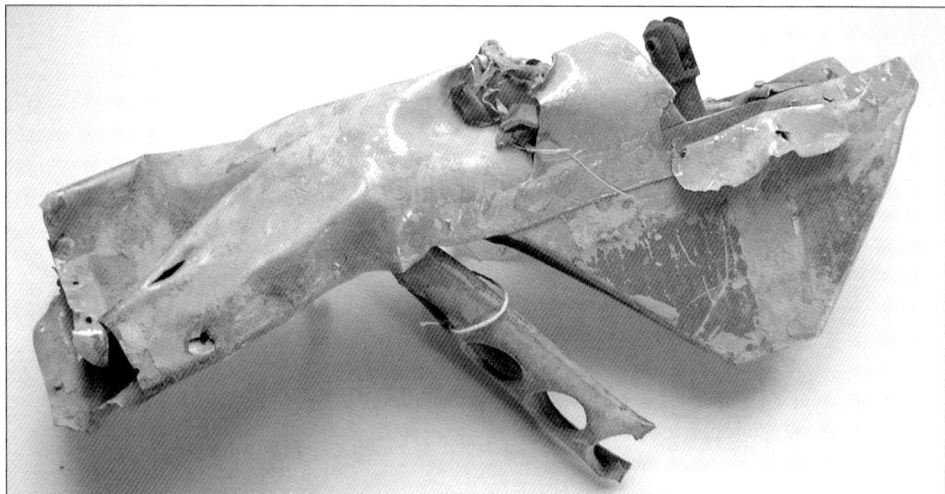

Above. This piece of tailplane structure has also retained some of its original paint - much of which is also red. This part comes from the Bf109E that crashed at Wickhambreux near Canterbury on the 7th September 1940.

Right. Finding part of the aircraft code or serial number helps provide the archaeologist with identification of a set of aircraft remains. This photograph shows a section of the fuselage from a Focke-Wolf 190 that was shot down on the 17th August 1943. Strictly this shouldn't be included within this book as the aircraft crashed in Belgium, following combat with a formation of B-17 bombers. However, it clearly shows part of the aircraft's code number that was once painted in the centre of its fuselage. In this case the number was a black 8! It is also interesting to note the white outline of the number and the surrounding standard green painted on Luftwaffe fighters of the period.

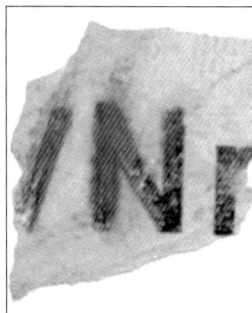

Left. In all digs much importance is placed on finding some indication of an aircraft's werke, or serial, number. Each aircraft would have its own werke number and it is this that helps an historian trace a particular aircraft's history and movement. It has not been unknown for the German quartermaster-general's records to be inaccurate and also for parts, such as engines, to be switched in the heat of battle, but finding evidence of the werke number in an excavation goes some way to proving beyond all doubt. This is actually a paint peeling that was taken from inside a part of the fuselage from a Bf109 unearthed during 1975. The inscription is part of the text 'W/Nr', an abbreviation for werke number. It was unfortunate that whilst this part could be saved the actual serial number that followed, which was '3874', could not be enticed off!

fighters. On the same day, Friday the 16th August 1940, Geoff approached the location along the footpath that heads south, away from the South Downs Way, at Chantry Hill carpark. His drawings provide us with some clue as to the damage inflicted on the aircraft by the RAF fighters. In the first of these two side views **(below)** he notes damage to the starboard engine and propellers and a bullet hole in the rear fuselage, whilst in the second, **(bottom)** observes that oil has sprayed across the tailplane. Interestingly, he also records evidence that prior to being shot down themselves, the crew had had some success in an earlier confrontation! (By kind permission of Mr. G. Goatcher)

Above. This small and almost insignificant fragment is an excellent example of how the excavation of a particular crash site might help provide the replies to some unanswered questions. On the 15th August 1940 a Messerschmitt Bf109E-4 was shot down whilst acting as escort to a group of Bf110s on a mission to bomb Croydon. The pilot, Lt. Marx, baled out and was captured, whilst the plane fell to the ground at Lightlands Farm, Frant. Despite much investigation and trolling through German records, the werke number for this aircraft was never found. A subsequent investigation of the crash site uncovered this small piece of aluminum. On it is stamped a four-digit number, which is believed to represent the missing serial number.

Right. There is one, albeit less common, source of information available to the aviation historian. This is the eyewitness drawing. The drawings here are the work of Geoff Goatcher who, as a young schoolboy, had no other means of recording what he saw. Throughout the Battle of Britain he lived in the village of Washington which, being on the South Downs, provided an excellent viewpoint from which to observe the dogfights that unfolded in the skies above him. On hearing of a crashed plane Geoff would jump on his bicycle and, pedaling furiously, make his way to the crash site. Once there he sketched, in full colour, what lay before him.

In these pictures Geoff has sketched the remarkably intact remains of a Bf110C that crashed at Lee Farm on the Downs at Clapham following contact with RAF

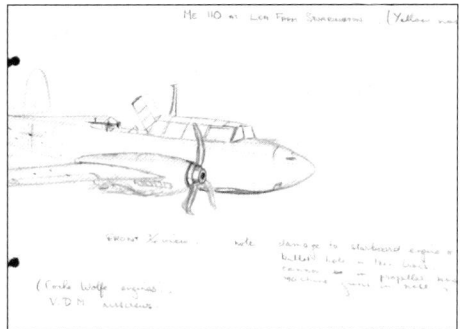

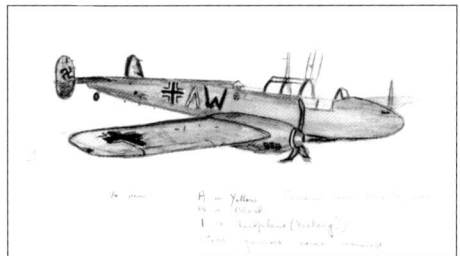

When using such drawings, a word of caution might be advisable. In his two 3/4 views Geoff shows the last part of the aircraft code letters as 'AW'. However, a photograph of the actual aircraft suggests something different. In this the letters appear as after the fuselage cross as 'AP'. The police report and other eyewitness testaments support this interpretation, which reveals the full code as 2N+AP. This discrepancy is probably due to the fact that Geoff, by his own admission, occasionally added the finishing touches to his drawings from memory when

having returned home. This photograph **(above)** also shows the remarkable condition in which the aircraft was left after the crash landing, with even the cockpit covers still in place. (By kind permission of Mr. A. Saunders)

In another of the aircraft crash sites that Geoff Goatcher visited he was able to sketch the, again remarkably intact, remains of a Bf109 **(below)**. This was the plane that was chased over Storrington on the 9th September 1940 only to crash land on the gliding field at Parham - see the book 'Chanctonbury Crashes'. As ever Geoff provides an insight into the damage inflicted on the aircraft by the two RAF fighters that, even as Oblt. Daig himself has recalled, doggedly pursued it. On the drawing is a note that states that a bullet had clearly hit, amongst other parts, the oil tank. Paradoxically, as a result of the aircraft's condition, Daig's 109 went on to support the British war effort in its fight against the Luftwaffe.

During the last months of 1940 dozens of towns and cities across the country participated in national 'War Weapons Week'. At the centre of many of these events were displays of captured German aircraft, the most popular of which were the Bf109. For about sixpence, (2½ pence), the public could stand and gaze at, or even climb into, an example of the Luftwaffe's finest. It is known that this 109 was part of these displays, having been photographed at events in Birmingham and Dudley, and therefore in its own little way helped buy a Spitfire! (By kind permission of Mr. G. Goatcher)

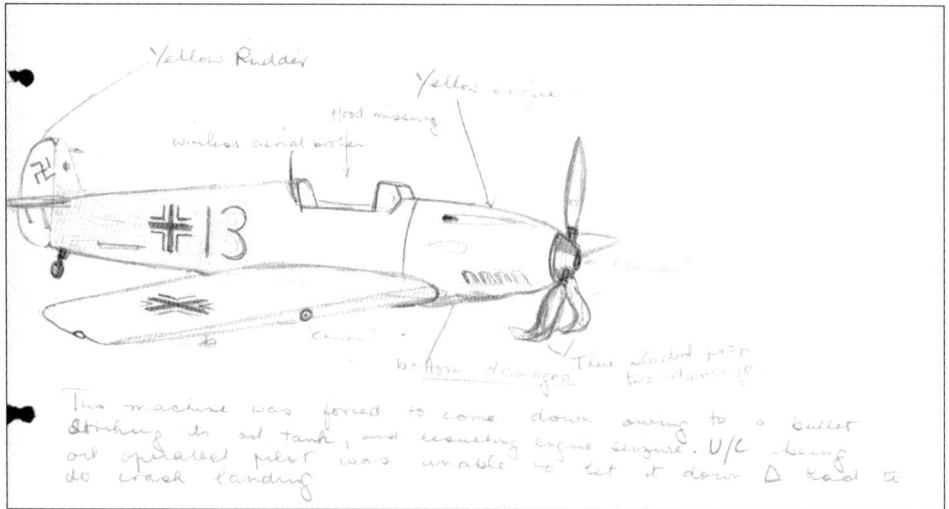

Above. Another section of tailplane from a Bf109, though this time from one with a rather unique history. It came from an aircraft that was to have the distinction of crashing not once, but twice onto British soil! The aircraft was a Bf109F-2, werke number

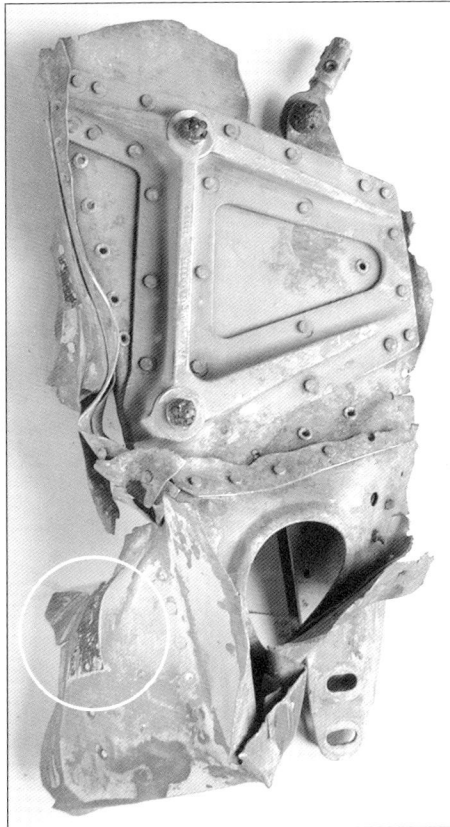

12764, that was flown by Gruppen Kommandeur Major Rolf Pingels of JG.26 and which, on the 10th July 1941, crash landed on the beach at St. Margaret's Bay, Dover. Quickly repaired, the aircraft was put back into the air by the Air Fighter Development Unit, (AFDU), with the RAF designation ES 906. Rigorous testing followed for the next two months before disaster happened. On the 20th October the same year, the fighter was taking part in comparative speed tests with a Spitfire when it crashed near Fowlmere airfield. Piloted on this occasion by a Pole, FO Skalski, the plane was seen diving towards the airfield with an increasingly steeper angle and speed. Eventually, hurtling vertically down, the aircraft ploughed into the ground. The cause of the crash was almost certainly oxygen failure. Skalski, who sadly died in the crash, was subsequently found to have 30% carbon monoxide in his blood, indicating that if he had not been unconscious at the moment of impact, he certainly would have been far from fully efficient. When the site was excavated it was found that some of the aircraft must have been removed in the days after the crash, no doubt at the time the authorities recovered Skalski's body. The parts that remained though included the engine, three propellers, tail wheel, radio set, the two main wheels and nearly all the fin and tailplanes - a part of which is shown here. One point worthy of note, noticed during the excavation, was the fact that much of the aircraft had been repainted yellow, indicating that this was a RAF test aircraft. It was also found that RAF roundels had been crudely added over the top of the swastikas on the fuselage.

Left. This section of a Bf109 flap frame shows how parts of an aircraft's markings can be found on recovered fragments. Whilst the surface mainly visible is in fact the inside of the flap, part of the exterior surface can still be seen bent over one of the edges. This outer surface still sports the characteristic olive drab green used by the Luftwaffe on the upper surfaces of many aircraft. Even more interestingly is the fact that part of the black cross still remains, (circled). This part, more correctly known as a 'de Havilland flap', originates from the Bf109 that crashed at Grayswood, Haslemere, on the 30th September 1940.

wreckage from a crashed Bf109 and not just a fishing weight! It is in fact a teardrop balance, and can be found under each wing on a Bf109. Indeed, if you look closely at the Hendon exhibit you will see one protruding from the trailing edge of any wing closest to you. Mounted on a small arm these somewhat innocuous devices helped maintain the balance of the ailerons. Cast from iron, each one was specific in weight to the aircraft to which it was fitted.

If you were able to turn over the example illustrated here, which was recovered from a Bf109 crash site at Appledore in Kent, you would find some of the original canvas covering still in place.

Bottom left. Having read the story of FO Skalski one immediately realises the importance of a good oxygen supply to a pilot. Here is the regulator that came from the Bf109, werke 5895, flown by Obfw. Gunther Struck. This aircraft crashed on the 24th April 1941 on an open field at Black House Farm, Camber near Rye.

Above. A visit to the Battle of Britain museum at Hendon will prove that this really is a piece of

All of the identification plates, dials and part numbers are still visible.

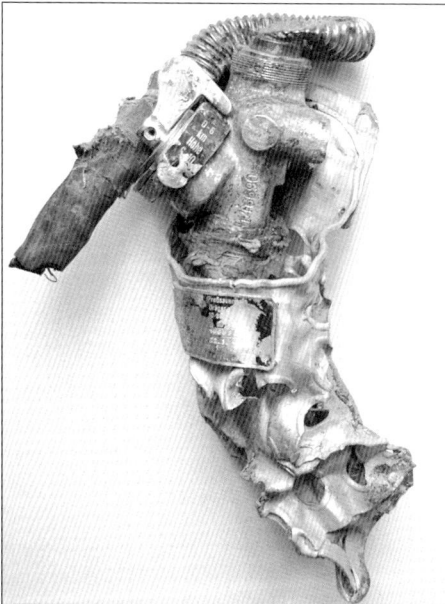

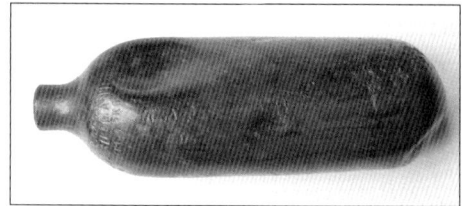

Above. Along with the regulator another of the somewhat vital parts of an oxygen supply system is the oxygen bottle itself! On the 25th August 1940 a Messerschmitt Bf110 was shot down following RAF fighter interception of an incoming German bomber force. This aircraft, werke number 3532, crashed at 5.30pm at Tatton House Farm, Buckland Ripers in Dorset. This bottle was recovered in the subsequent excavation of the site, and is in such a remarkable condition that the markings stamped on the side are easily read. Manufactured by a company called 'Friedmann', it had a capacity of 6kg.

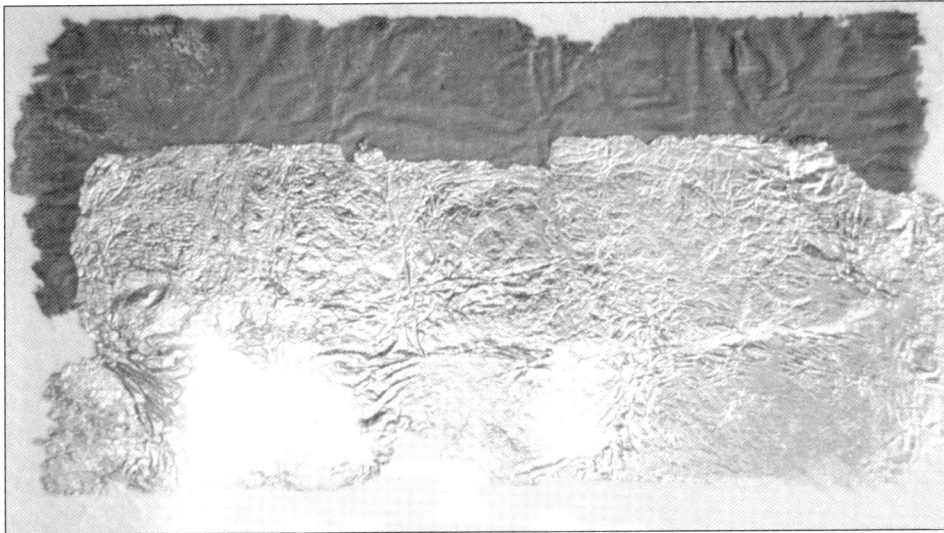

Above. No, this is not a chewing gum wrapper! It is in fact part of the padding and heat insulation from the pipework of a Bf109. The Messerschmitt concerned, a 109E-4 from the 3rd Staffel JG52, was abandoned during a dogfight after being intercepted by RAF fighters. The aircraft had been acting as escort to some fighter-bombers that had been attempting to bomb the airfield at Biggin Hill. The pilot, Voss, landed unhurt, whilst the plane fell out of control. It impacted at The Limes, Brabourne Down, near Ashford in Kent.

Slightly bent as a result of the impact of the crash, this (**right**) is a machine gun mounting from a Bf109. The excavation that uncovered this relic was on the aircraft that crashed at Merthersham near Rye.

Each Bf109 (depending upon the model) had two nose mounted machine guns located above the engine, and in turn each of the machine guns would have been fixed in place by two of these mountings. The machine guns were the 7.92mm Rheinmetall-Borsig MG-17 type **(below)**.

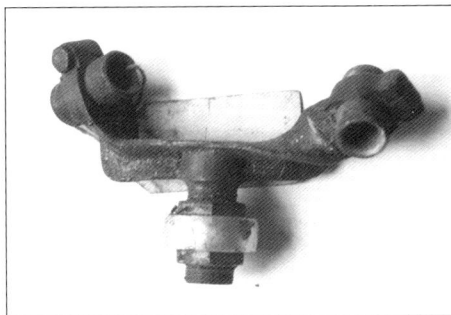

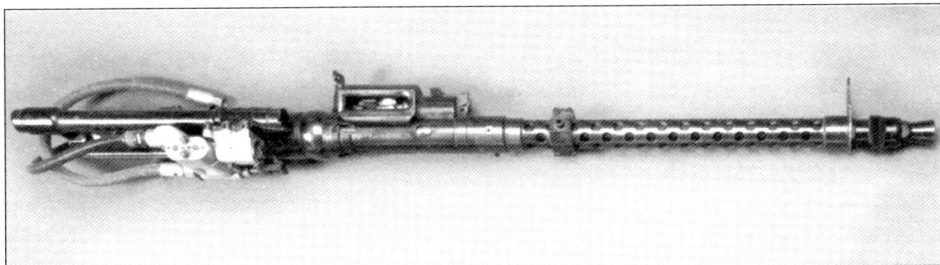

Above. Frequently an excavation would provide a surprise or two. This illustration of a recovered wartime Luftwaffe map could be just such an example. Clearly marked in the centre of the map is an airfield, indicated by the purple aircraft silhouette that the Luftwaffe cartographers used to show a 'Flugplatz'. What is surprising here is the location - named simply as Gumber Farm. Gumber Farm can be found on the Roman road, Stane Street, which crosses the South Downs north of Chichester in West Sussex. A quick glance at any list of wartime airfields shows that no such airfield ever existed here. It appears that the Germans were successfully deceived, for Gumber Farm was the location of a decoy airfield site. Identified as K.51, Gumber Farm was a KQ site, meaning that it was fitted out for both day and night decoy operations. Work started on the site in 1940, and by the end of that year it was fully operational. For the night-time deception a false flare path was put in place and arranged like the lights of its parent airfield at Tangmere. For the daytime, wooden decoy aircraft were scattered around the 'runway' - a grass field that ran across Stane Street. These wooden aircraft, designed by film set designers from Elstree Studios, took the Hawker Hurricane as their basis. They were built by a garden furniture manufacturer, at a price of £50 each, in Hailsham, East Sussex. From this map historians can deduce that, at some point in the war, the deception must have worked. Why else would the Luftwaffe indicate an airfield in such an isolated part of West Sussex?!

(By kind permission of the West Sussex Record Office)

Above. Another superb casting similar to that on page 8. Strictly speaking this excellent model has a two-tier history. The casting itself was made some years after the war, though very obviously to an incredibly high, and detailed, standard. It is the source of the metal used that is of particular interest. Early in the evening of Thursday the 15th August 1940 a German bomber formation tried to force its way through to Croydon airfield. Challenged by RAF fighters, some seven 110s were shot down. One of these crashed in flames at Bletchinglye Farm, Rotherfield. Subsequently excavated, a large amount of melted engine alloy was found amongst the parts recovered from the site. Being visually anonymous an idea was put forward to make use of these lumps and chunks. This beautiful model of a Bf110 was the result.

Bottom. Thirty six years after one particular aircraft crash, play was once again forced to stop on the golf course at Cannons Hill, Coulsdon in Surrey - same place, same plane. The story began early on the morning of Friday the 6th September 1940. Following a brief but frantic dogfight over Brooklands racecourse, RAF fighters claimed victory as one of the attacking Messerschmitt Bf110s spun away, obviously out of control. One of the crew, Uffz. Neusz, was seen to bale out and survived to be captured. At 9.30am the aircraft, with remaining crew member Uffz. Kiehn still inside, crashed into one of the greens at Cannons Hill Golf Course. In 1976 diggers once again returned to the site. Here they can be seen battling in the almost obligatory muddy trench in an effort to excavate what remains of Bf110 werke 2146.

Below. A quite impressive array of remains were recovered from under the Golf Course. Had the original RAF clearance team been wary of making too much of a mess of the greens back in 1940?

Shown here are three of the six propellers that were fitted to each 110. Also seeing daylight once again were both of the engines, both undercarriage legs and tyres, the complete set of armaments, tail wheel and, somewhat surprisingly, the port tail fin still with glimpses of the Swastika present. Also of interest in this instance was the fact that extensive remains from within the cockpit area were unearthed - Kiehn's parachute, sadly still folded and unused; the pilot's 1940 diary; and even the entire first aid kit. Somewhat gruesome was the discovery that the latter contained a number of surgical instruments - including a bone saw!

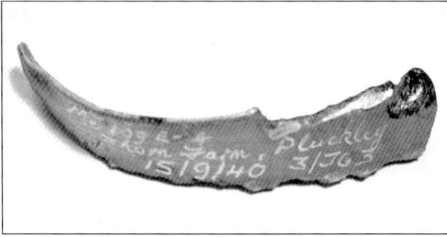

Above. Finding entire propeller blades during the course of an excavation is not always the norm. They were frequently recovered at the time as one of the most sought after trophies. Often a 'dig' will fail to yield such items, though in a few instances parts of a single blade might be found. This small fragment is a perfect example. As a Bf109 crashed at Thorn Farm, Pluckley in Kent, on the 15th September 1940, this small shard must have been sheared off the side of one of the propellers either by another part of the aircraft or by something in the ground. Whatever the cause, having been nicked off the shard fell away to be subsequently found in the excavation near the surface. The pilot, Oblt. Reumschuessel, had baled out and was captured unhurt. He must have been in the practice of taking his helmet off during flight, or had time to remove it before leaving his cockpit, for remains of this and his oxygen mask were recovered during the dig.

Top right. As we have seen, markings and colouring on relics from an aircraft's exterior can prove helpful in establishing its identity. Similar inferences may sometimes be drawn when examining a range of mechanical parts. With years worth of experience in the field of aviation archaeology, many enthusiasts, such as Pat Burgess, are able to suggest the origin within an aircraft of a particular fragment by studying its colour. The item shown here is a good example, though the fact that the picture is reproduced in black and white does not help. Pulled from the crash site of a Bf110 this piece, still clearly sporting its part number, was cleaned up and found to have been completely painted red - except for a couple of the brass fittings. It is in fact a junction in the oil piping from the plane, and it is thought that parts painted red are connected with the 110s oil system. Note the oil temperature sensor that has been unscrewed on one side.

Below. Continuing our tour of the mechanicals of a Bf110 is this item recovered from the crash site at Toat Hill, Pulborough in West Sussex. This time it is a piece of the pipe-work connected to the water coolant system. Sections from this network seemed to have routinely been painted green - as is the case here. Again the part numbers have been clearly cast onto the side of the pipe.

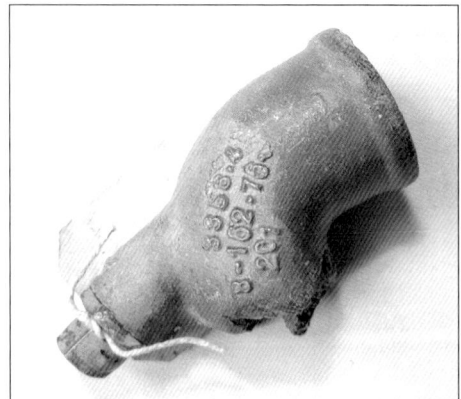

Above. One of the larger pieces included in this book - a radiator flap from a Bf109. It was one of the items recovered during the excavation of the crash site at Lidham Hall Farm - see page 4. This radiator outlet flap would have been located underneath the aircraft's nose, beneath the engine. It had a relatively simple task - controlling the flow of cooling air into the radiator cowling. Two points are worthy of note. Firstly that some of the original paintwork still remains, and secondly that the hole on the bottom left, (circled), is crash damage and not a bullet hole.

Below. Here we can see another relic from the sharp end of a Bf109! It is in fact one of the exhaust ejector stubs. Each 109 had 5 of these facing rearwards on each side of the engine behind an exhaust forward fairing. Many feel that these stubs help give the nose of the 109 its characteristic appearance. This example was recovered from the remains of a 109 that was shot down on the 18th August 1940. At this time the Battle of Britain was at its peak, and the 18th was a day of bloody action. The Luftwaffe saw some 53 aircraft lost in action (the RAF suffered 31), a figure that forced a radical change of policy on Hitler and Goering. Stunned by such a loss of aircraft and pilots in a single day the Luftwaffe's moral slumped to a new low, strengthened by the disparity between the assurances of their leaders and the reality of RAF Fighter Commands performance. This was the day that the invasion of Britain was postponed for the first time. Squadron Leader Pemberton, flying a Hurricane from No 1 Squadron based at Northolt, helped secure this decision - a definite member of 'The Few'. At 6.15pm he engaged a Bf109E-4 over Sussex. The plane burned out having hit the ground at Blue House Farm, Milebush in East Sussex. Also recovered in the 1981 excavation of this location was an undercarriage door, leading edge of one of the wings and a complete front section of cockpit canopy frame. Squadron Leader Pemberton was killed before he got the chance to see the final allied victory he had helped achieve.

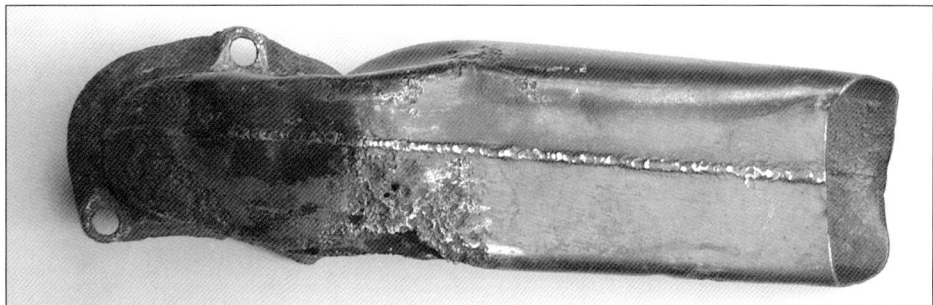

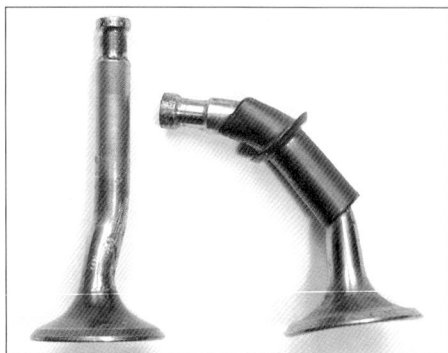

Above left. This crankshaft shell bearing comes from the crash site of a Bf109 that, for some reason, has been frequently visited. One of the first was by a group of unknown enthusiasts who left remains scattered around the area - much to the consternation of the local council.

The site is in Bishopden Wood, near Dunkirk in Kent, and the aircraft a 109E-1 which was shot down by an RAF fighter during a dogfight over northern Kent. One fact worth noting, though totally unconnected with the direct topic in hand concerns the ball bearings themselves. Examination of many wartime bomber command target sheets often reveals the bland explanation 'ball bearing factory'. Ball bearings such as those illustrated here were crucial in keeping the mechanicals of the German war machine rolling and so their manufacture frequently became the subject of an RAF bomb load!

Above right. One of the most sought after finds from an excavation - engine valves. These examples are from two different crash sites. The straighter one on the left was found among the remains of the Bf110 that crashed at Toat Hill, Pulborough (page 18). The bent right hand specimen came from the Claytons Farm dig near Peasmarsh. This valve still has retained part of its bronze sleeve.

Above. Another hole, another 'dig', and another set of remains from the 15th August 1940. It is 1993 and the dig is well underway though, for once, in dry chalk and not clinging mud. The target is a Bf110C that crashed at Slackstead Manor, Hursley, near Winchester. Very quickly the mechanical digger provided the first signs of a successful excavation - both of the aircraft's Daimler-Benz engines. These were remarkably complete, with the propeller hubs still attached minus the propellers themselves. All the wreckage was badly burnt, telling the archaeologists that the plane burnt out in the hours during and after the crash. Two 20mm cannons and a bucket load of ammunition were also brought to the surface. One highly interesting discovery was around the 20mm cannon access panel. Here red paintwork indicated the presence of the characteristic shark's mouth emblem of ZG 76 - the unit in which this particular 110 had served.

TIONS')s—

HE FELL ON SUSSEX—
*The final second—and one more
Battle of Britain is over*

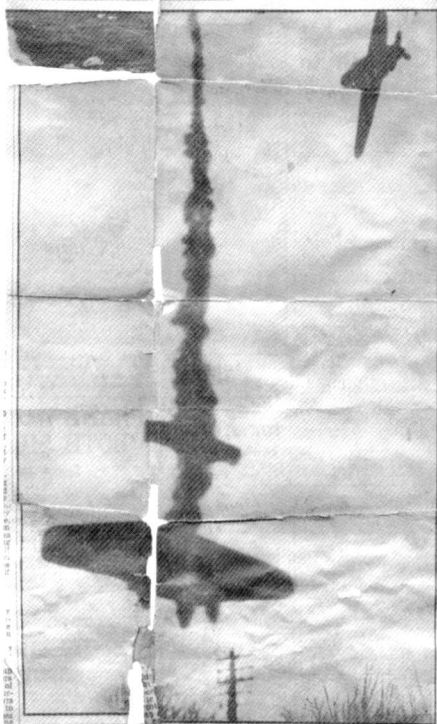

HERE is the plane-crash picture of the year . . . the incident often described rare? photographed : .. rain A German bomber falls to earth at Goodwood, Sussex, drawing its funeral plume behind. The fighter that shot it down follows almost to telegraph-pole height to establish its finish, and for that split-second finish a Daily Express reader had a camera and presence of mind.

The raider came to England on a daylight trip last month— when fewer enemies came than in any month this year. It was one of the 18 July raiders that did not return.

TO CRASH.....OR NOT TO CRASH!

This newspaper cutting, from a national daily newspaper, shows a remarkable photograph that was taken on the 18th July 1940 during the height of the Battle of Britain. As can be seen in the caption **(below left)** it depicts the end of a German twin-engined aircraft, such as a Messerschmitt Bf110, over Goodwood in West Sussex. However, appearances can be deceptive for things are not quite as they seem!

Despite the fact that the 'Battle' was only eight days old by the 18th, it proved to be a quiet day. The weather was miserable with cloud over most of the country and showers in the south. There was some isolated activity - the Goodwin lightship was bombed and sunk; the coastguard station at St. Margaret's Bay in Kent was hit and shipping in the Channel suffered from uncoordinated incursions. There was only one major engagement when some 15 Spitfires intercepted twenty-eight Bf109s. How then did this Bf110 become a victim so far away from the activity over eastern Kent?

Further head scratching occurs if you check the official German loss reports for the 18th. On this Thursday the Luftwaffe lost a total of twelve aircraft. One was a single engined Bf109 and can be counted out. A further eight were lost over the European mainland, usually as a result of battle damage picked up in operations over Britain, or due to an accident. That leaves the historian with three possible aircraft. Two were Junkers Ju88 bombers, and the last a Dornier Do 17. It is here that the plot thickens, for both of these aircraft types are bigger than the aircraft shot down in this photograph.

The truth behind this 'gallant victory' is unravelled in the amazing, and almost unbelievable, story of a Sussex teenager, Ron Cripps. At this point in the war Ron was living at home with his parents awaiting his call up into the RAF. Indeed, by the middle of 1941 his personal papers show he was serving as a L.A.C. technician in Bomber Command. One day, perhaps whilst bored and looking for something to pass the time, Ron decided to take his collection of model aircraft out into the garden. Finding some loose bits of cotton thread he had the bright idea of hanging the various aircraft from his mother's washing line! The result can be seen in the picture **(right)**, as a gaggle of various British aircraft types dangle in the midday sun! The washing line, arrowed, can be seen quite clearly.

At some point about now, Ron had the idea of taking his diorama one stage further. He cleared the line, leaving only his model of a Hurricane and a British twin engined type **(centre right)**. By using a bit more cotton thread, and some other household items, he stepped back to admire his efforts. Impressed, he reached for his Dad's camera and used up the last of the families remaining pre-war supply of film. When developed the final result, **(bottom right)**, looked remarkably realistic - perhaps too much so!

There it was - a model kit hanging by cotton thread from a washing line! Cotton wool twisted around the string provided the flames whilst the victorious RAF fighter swung lazily a bit higher up. In the background could be seen the telegraph pole at the bottom of the garden. This garden, however, was nowhere near Goodwood. Ron's family then lived in a house called 'Greenhedges' which was just outside the Sussex village of Storrington. Whilst the house has long since been demolished, this telegraph pole can still be seen near the junction of Greenhurst Lane and the West Chiltington Road!

The only unanswered part of this story is how a picture of a teenager's models could become part of the national headlines. Ron himself cannot provide the answer, for he only found out how his pictures had been used by accident. Reading a friends paper, he almost fainted with surprise on turning the page to see his models spread before him on the paper. Were duplicates made when the negatives were developed? Did someone sell these copies on - Ron still has all the original photographs in his possession. Whatever the truth, perhaps this tale is another reminder of the fact that you cannot always believe what the papers say - particularly after a country's wartime propaganda machine has been in full swing. (All pictures by kind permission of Mr. Ron Cripps and his family)

Above. Another fragment that provides the enthusiast with precise information. Here is part of the engine casing of a Daimler-Benz DB601 engine uncovered at Toat Hill near Pulborough. Cast into it is a host of specific details. Reading from the top down we can deduce that the engine was built on the 11th August 193?, was of the 601 type, and that it had been given the specific serial number 3205. The DB601 engine was a remarkable unit that eventually powered both the Bf109 and Bf110. Installation of this engine into the Bf109 from 1938 onwards transformed its performance from plain good to excellent. The introduction of direct fuel injection meant that the German designers had side stepped

the problem of fuel supply cutouts experienced with normal float carburettors. This therefore enabled the 109 to completely out dive any contemporary British fighter of the time. Equally, the DB601 produced 1,175hp at take-off, making this more powerful than the Merlin engines in the Hurricanes and Spitfires supplied to the RAF at this point of the war.

Staying with engines and the Toat Hill crash, **above right** is a part of the supercharger fitted to each of the aircraft's engines. By their very nature engine parts were manufactured to be robust and strong, and therefore they are common finds in most aircraft excavations.

Left. This well-preserved engine plate represents a good find for any 'dig'. From it we can glean as much detail as from the DB601 engine block casing shown above. We can prove that the aircraft was fitted with a Daimler-Benz unit, which type and what serial it carried. Interestingly we also get an insight into the manufacturer of this particular power plant. Initially the 601 was manufactured solely by Daimler-Benz at its plants in Genshagen and Marienfelde. As demand spiraled, further production lines were set up at other companies such as Henschel and Bussing-Werke. This plate tells us that Henschel Flugmotorenbau built the engine at its Kassell works.

23

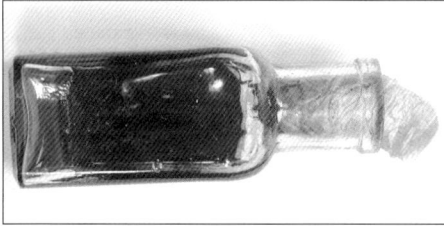

Above. Sometimes an excavation would throw up a particular relic to surprise the aviation archaeologist. Brought down by RAF fighters, Messerschmitt Bf109, werke 3874, plunged to earth near St. Nicholas-at-Wade, Kent. Burying itself to a depth of between 30 and 40 feet the remains of this aircraft lay entombed and untouched until 1975. As the aviation archaeologists dug down they came across part of the engine block. Still resting in it was a pool of a black liquid. Feeling that further investigation was needed, some of this 'treacle' was scooped out and bottled. Samples were sent for analysis, and it was found that the liquid was in fact engine oil. More surprising was that the tests went further and indicated that the oil was in perfect condition - as good as the day it was first refined! Needless to say, the bottle here is not an original relic, only the oil within.

Right. This single seat biplane is the only relic included in this book that is not German. It is in fact a Fiat CR.42 from the Italian Air Force, the Regia Aeronautica. Whilst a sheer delight to fly, this type was obsolete the very moment the first of the 1,784 total built rolled off the production lines. It proved to be totally outclassed by the British Spitfires and Hurricanes. Nevertheless, the Regia Aeronautica did operate over the United Kingdom. One group of 50 CR.42s provided the fighter element of the Corpo Aereo Italiano, which operated from bases in Belgium. Their activity over Southern England, predominantly between October 1940 and January 1941, was marked by a conspicuous lack of success. This example was shot down by Hurricanes from Martlesham Heath during an attack on the 11th November 1940. Suffering a fractured oil pipe its pilot force landed on the beach at Orfordness, Suffolk, without suffering any further damage. Allocated the RAF serial number BT 474, the aircraft then passed through several evaluation and research departments. Perhaps one of the most important of these was the Air Fighting Development Unit, (AFDU), based at Duxford. Here the Fiat was flown extensively to help develop tactics against the type, which was then the standard Italian fighter in use in the Middle East. In 1943 this airframe was recognised as a valuable museum piece and saved from destruction. In 1979 it came to its final resting-place where this picture was taken - the RAF Museum at Hendon. (By kind permission of the RAF Museum)

Left. As already mentioned, finding pools of engine oil is quite a rarity. More commonly, lubricants are found in sealed units that survived a crash intact. Being large, heavy, lumps engines often broke up or, at the very least, cracked during a crash thereby allowing oil to escape. This would still manifest itself many years later, but in the manner shown in this picture. Here a deep trench uncovers the buried remains of the Bf110 that crashed at North Baddesley in Hampshire. As the mechanical digger exposes one of the undercarriage legs and wheel, (circled), with its whole tyre still attached, the on-looker can see the characteristic black staining of the soil caused by the aircraft's engine oil seeping out in the years after the crash.

Above. Frequently when a cockpit clock is unearthed in the course of a 'dig' it is found to have stopped at the time of the crash, assisting the historian in timing the incident. The fascinating piece illustrated here is a find to the contrary. The whole ensemble is in fact made up from parts found at two different sites. The base, a mixture of a bearing ring and gear cogs, was sourced from the remains of the Bf110 crash on Cannons Hill Golf Course in Coulsdon. Meanwhile the clock, expertly mounted on a block of polished oak, was found as the result of a fighter interception carried out by Flying Officer Nelson of No. 74 Squadron. The day before the end of the Battle of Britain, October 29th 1940, he shot down a Bf109 that flew into the ground at Dodds Farm, Langton. In the subsequent excavation, the clock was found still resting in part of the original cockpit dashboard. Unlike similar finds, turn the winder and this clock starts ticking again!

Cockpit finds can often be of a more personal nature, as the next few pictures will illustrate. One of the most famous images of the Battle of Britain is the photograph showing the remains of a Bf110 that crashed into the pond in front of Shopwycke House, near Tangmere. The date was the 16th August 1940. This section of a pair of scissors **(above right)** was found amongst the wreckage from that aircraft which was uncovered in 1978. The scissors almost certainly originate from the first aid kit which was stored in the cockpit.

Paper based finds are less common. Burning wreckage, burial and exposure to the elements do nothing to support the longevity of such items. Occasionally an excavation might throw up a map or diary, but the item shown here is even rarer.

In the Appledore 'dig' this distinctly battered and faded 100 Reichmark bank note **(below)** was again brought out into the glare of daylight. Its original owner, Lt. Strobel, unfortunately never lived to spend it in the pilot's mess.

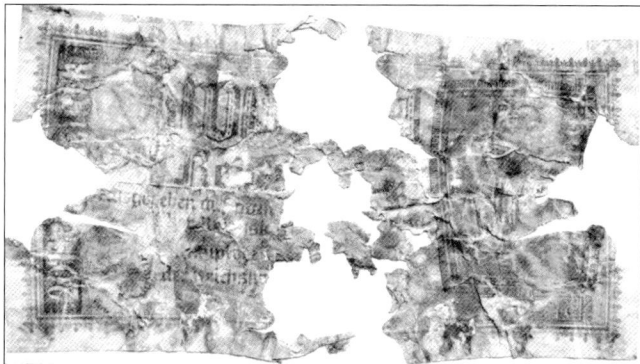

Even rarer than finding a banknote is the discovery of a stamp **(below)**. Burial and passage of time has meant that this relic really is in poor condition, and is almost unrecognizable - it was found in the same part of the Appledore 109 cockpit as the 100 Reichmark note.

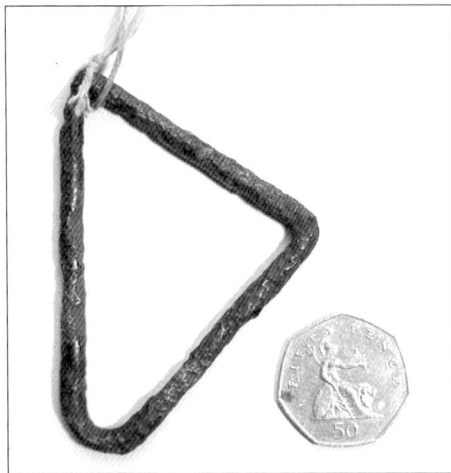

Above. Another of Geoff Goatcher's sketches, with a different 110 as the inspiration. Wednesday the 4th September 1940 was a day of carnage for the 3rd Staffel ZG76. In the space of a few hours they lost four aircraft over the Sussex Downs. One of these, werke number 3563, was shot down by P/O Moody as the Germans tried to press home an attack on the radar station at Poling. Mortally hit by a 602 Squadron Spitfire, the Bf110 crash landed at Strivens Farm, near Steyning in West Sussex. As well as a 3/4 view, Geoff also penned what was visible inside the cockpit - including the two seats from which the previous seat harness fixing would have belonged. (By kind permission of Mr. G. Goatcher)

Bottom. Close examination of the spoil from any excavation site is vital. Without such attention to detail this fragment from a 110 that crashed at Bletchinglye Farm, Rotherfield, on the 15th August 1940, would have been missed. A fifty pence piece has been added to illustrate just how small it actually is. Careful thought after the dig also revealed its purpose - part of a cockpit seat harness fixing.

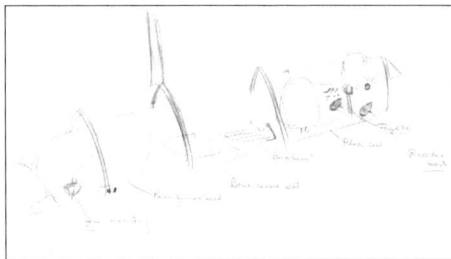

Right. Having said that paper stands the test of time badly, this is yet another example to the contrary! Recovered on the 12th August 1981, from the Bf110 that crashed at Buckland Ripers, Dorset, no one is actually sure of its origin. The favorite is the possibility that it is a cigar or cigarette paper.

Frequently a part or fragment cannot be identified at the time of the excavation. Subsequent reference to specialist publications, line

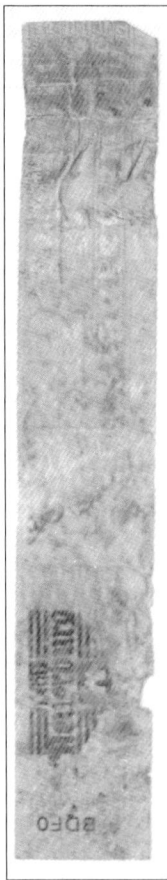

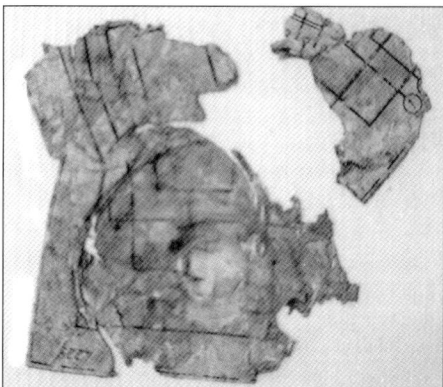

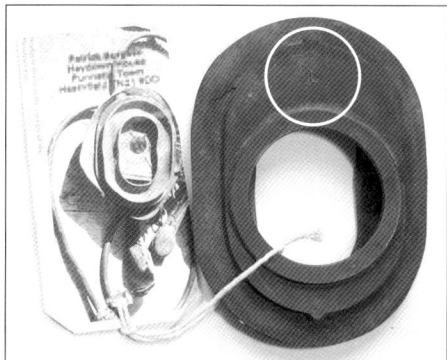

drawings or a more knowledgeable colleague is a common occurrence. For a number of years this relic **(above)** passed unidentified. Indeed it came close to being thrown out on a number of occasions. All that was known was that it was recovered from the cockpit area of a Bf109 that crashed near Cross-in-Hand, East Sussex, on the 7th October 1940, and that it bore the letter 'L' near the top, (circled). The chance reading of an imported Eastern European magazine provided the answer. As seen from the tag attached to the relic the answer became clear. What had been unearthed was in fact the inner left ear pad from the pilot's flying helmet!

Parts of the radio and communication systems from an individual aircraft are regular finds. Two examples are illustrated here. The first **(below)** shows fragments of a wiring diagram recovered from the cockpit of a 109, whilst the second **(above right)** is part of the porcelain insulator that supported an aircraft's aerial. The latter was found in the excavation of a Bf110 that crashed at Clearhedge Farm, near Horam in East Sussex.

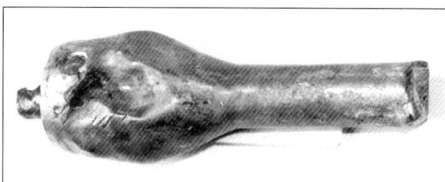

Above. The source of this item is, once again, the Bf109 that crashed at Methersham Bridge near Rye. Most people would have absolutely no indication as to its purpose. The solution, though, can be found by the close examination of any high quality cut-away drawing of a Bf109. Look at the bottom of the pilot's seat on its left-hand side and there is your answer, protruding up from the cockpit floor. It is in fact the seat adjustment lever!

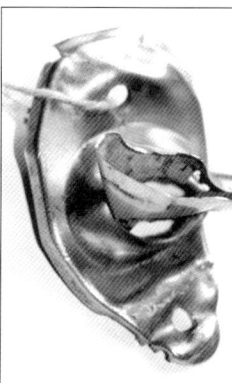

Left. Another poser from the same crash site, and the again the answer is found in the same way. Located at the very tip of each wing is a navigation light. This is the actual light bulb fitment, though the bulb itself has failed, somewhat unsurprisingly, to survive the crash!

crash, which cost the lives of both crew-members, had been a particularly violent one. It was then noticed that in one part of the ploughed field the concentration of fragments was higher. The mechanical digger went to work in this area. As the trench reached a depth of some eight feet the most significant find of the excavation was uncovered - enthusiast Pat Burgess is shown **left** with this relic. It is one of the two propeller hubs that were fitted, the other found as the digging worked out in a radius from this point. The only other significant item unearthed was a blast tube from one of the 20mm cannons. A number of representative pieces were retained, all showing a light grey colour.

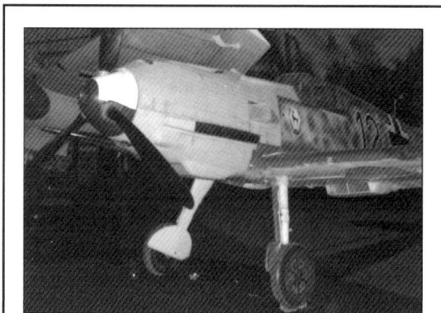

Saturday the 5th October 1940 was a damp, wet day with only the occasional bright spell. Throughout the day, the Luftwaffe had launched limited strikes at Southampton and Folkestone harbours, and the airfield at Detling. Fighter-bombers were also set upon London. In amongst the latter was a Bf110D-3 with the werke number 3383. As the two crew, Fw. Duensnig and Fw. Keppitsch, made their way northwards little did they know how bad their day was about to become. As Squadron Leader Hogan steered 501 Squadron in for attack, he took their plane in his sight. Following several direct hits the German aircraft fell out of control towards the ground, eventually crashing at Willowbeds Farm, near Ashford. The time was 11.30 am, and already the Luftwaffe was close to its total of nine aircraft lost on that day. Nearly fifty years were to pass before, on the 23rd August 1987, the site was once again opened up. Pieces were found to have been scattered over a very wide area, suggesting that the

Coded 'Black 12' this Messerschmitt Bf109E-3 **(above)** is the second of our whole aircraft relics which, like the Fiat Cr.42, is also on display in the RAF Museum. It force landed at Manston on the 27th November 1940 following combat with a patrol of Spitfires. It was made airworthy again by cannibalizing parts from other crashed 109s, and followed the Fiat through a whole host of evaluation tests.

This included some time spent with Rolls-Royce for engine performance tests, completing 32 flights totaling 23 hours and 25 minutes, and de Havilland at Hatfield for evaluation of the variable pitch propeller. By 1943 it had been replaced in the trials by newer examples and was relegated to travelling the country on fund raising exhibitions. (By kind permission of the Royal Air Force Museum)

Right. Not all crash sites give up such a wealth of information. It was late in the afternoon on Saturday the 24th August 1940, when a frantic dogfight broke out in the skies over the Isle of Wight. One of the casualties, a Bf-109E-4 from 6/JG.2, fell to earth in a heavily wooded copse at Shanklin Down. The pilot, Fw. Ebus, parachuted into the sea at Ventnor Bay, but sadly drowned before he could be rescued. Like the pilot, the aircraft also fell into water - at the bottom of an old, 80ft deep, Victorian water borehole! The subsequent excavation of this site must rank as one of the most extensive ever undertaken. Over several days three mechanical diggers were used in relays to dig into the steep hillside. The picture shows one of the JCBs attempting to reach the bottom of the well. Ton after ton of sandstone was removed in this massive operation to reach the bottom of the shaft. Despite such a huge effort only the occasional piece of small wreckage came to light. A few fragments were found in the well shaft itself, whilst others were scattered around at the top of the well. Indeed, the largest item that was recovered was one of the 20mm cannons.

Throughout the Second World War, Tangmere was the controlling, or sector station for 'A' Sector of No. 11 Group, Fighter Command. With its origins stretching as far back as 1916, Tangmere was to become as famous as its counterparts at Biggin Hill and Kenley. Like the Squadrons who flew from there, the airfield infrastructure was not to escape unscathed. The runways, hangers and other assorted buildings suffered particularly after the Luftwaffe's change of tactics during the Battle of Britain. Realising that they were failing to wipe out the fighter aircraft themselves, in August 1940, Goering ordered that his bombers now target their home bases. These two pictures, **left**, show some of the effects of these attacks. Both are accomodation blocks for airmen who were stationed at Tangmere, and which can still be seen north of the old runways in the village itself, (they are now surrounded by a new housing estate). Note that all the walls have been liberally peppered by machine gun fire and shrapnel strikes. The repair work is identical to that described on page 32. What is interesting, is that it is possible to tell where large chunks of shrapnel or flying debris have hit the walls - circled. Here new bricks have been used to plug the hole created, before the ubquitous wet concrete was added. (By kind permission of Mr. A. Oliver).

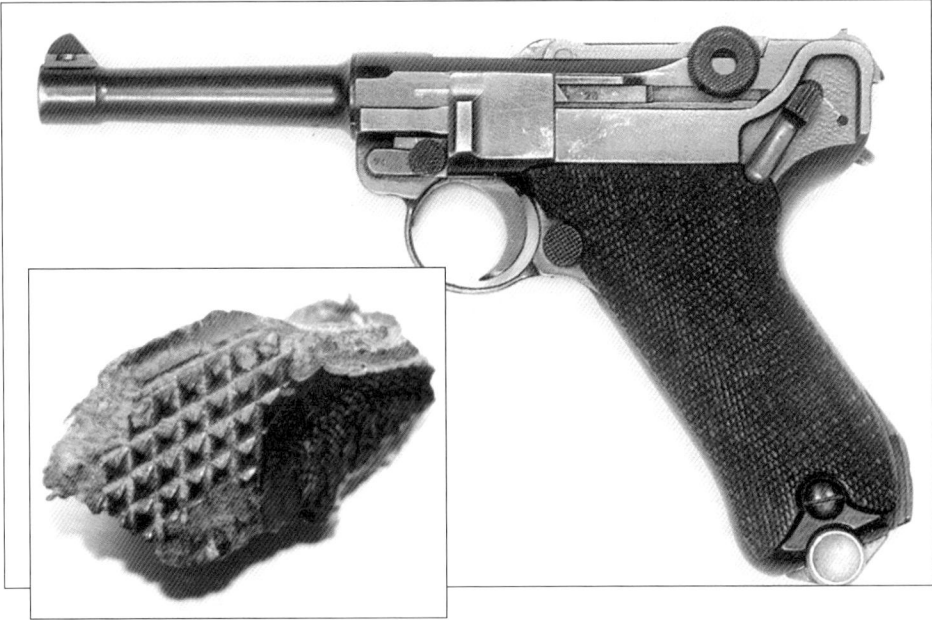

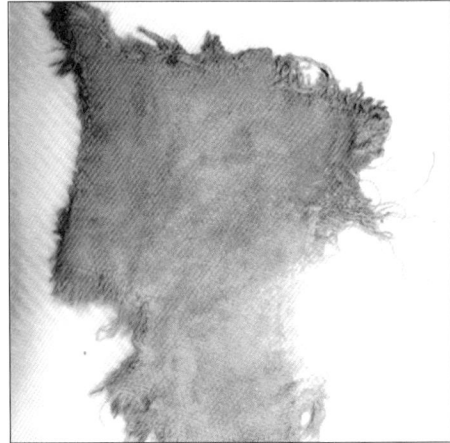

The grooves on this small fragment, **(above)**, provide the clues as to its function. Recovered from the remains of a Bf110 that crashed at Bletchinglye Farm, Rotherfield, on the 15th August 1940, this is believed to be a piece of the butt from a Luger pistol. Part of the standard uniform issue to Luftwaffe pilots and crew, the pistol was supposed to be carried in a leather holster worn on the left-hand side of the belt. Individual preferences often meant that the pistol might not be carried at all, or left loose somewhere in the cockpit.

The Luger, or more correctly the Luger Parabellum P08, began its development in 1900. The first country to adopt it was in fact Switzerland followed, in 1908, by the German Army. By the Second World, the P08 was standard issue for all arms of the German Armed Forces.

It was a reliable and well-made weapon, and many millions were produced by the time production ceased in 1942. The butt of this example (taken from a crashed aircraft in France and now in a French collection) shows the same pattern of grooves as the fragment illustrated.

Something of a mystery now. This fragment of canvas like material **(above)** was recovered from the Coulsdon crash site described on page 17. It is believed to have been found amongst remains that were recovered from the cockpit area. Could it be part of some webbing, a piece of seat fabric or all that remains of the pilot's personal kit bag? This small fragment probably looks larger than it actually is, only being a few inches across.

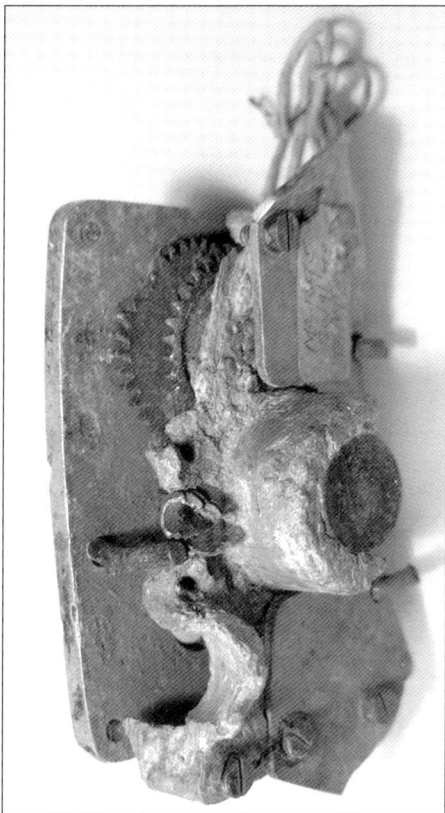

Left. This small, and to most people unrecognisable relic, is a part of the propeller pitch control system from a Bf109 that so interested de Havilland during their evaluation of the 'Hendon 109'. More specifically, this is a pitch adjuster control. Having a variable pitch propeller system brought with it the advantages of controlling the power supplied by an aircraft's engine, enhancing your level flight, take-off, landing and, off course, manoeuvrability characteristics. This part did not come from 'Black 12', but was recovered along with the propeller boss and engine parts, from the Bf109E-4 that crashed on the 30th September 1940 at Claytons Farm, Peasmarsh in East Sussex.

Bottom left. Like those made from card and paper, fabric remains are also relatively uncommon. This example, which does seem in surprising condition, is another recovery from the Lidham Hall Bf109. Called by a different term depending on whom you are talking to, it is essentially an 'entry foothold'. Reach for the cutaway drawing and you will find it on the left-hand side of the fuselage just behind the trailing edge of the wing. It is basically a foothold by which the pilot can lift himself onto the wing and then, from there, climb into the cockpit. The open end faces outwards and would normally be protected by a spring-loaded flap - this failed to survive the crash. Two of the rivets that originally held the step in place to a reinforced fuselage panel, can still be seen.

Below. In this detail added to one of his sketches, Geoff Goatcher illustrates an entry foothold from one of the aircraft he visited - the Bf110 that crashed at Lee Farm, Clapham, on the 16th August 1940. Note the similarities in design and position between those fitted to the 109 **(left)**, and the 110.

(By kind permission of Mr. G. Goatcher)

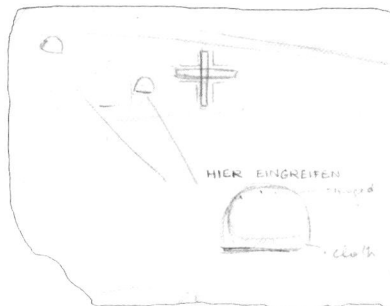

HIER EINGREIFEN

cloth

Right. Hidden away in the West Sussex countryside are the remains of the wartime radar station at Poling. The Air Ministry living quarters, now private housing, are still standing. Aerial photographs of the site whilst it was still in use clearly show that these buildings had an unhealthy proximity to the large transmitter towers. The degree of closeness can be seen from this picture - even now the houses show the scars of having been bombed and machine-gunned. At the time these scars, some caused by strafing German fighters, were simply filled with wet concrete that left them all too visible. Whilst in use the radar station provided much mystery for local people. When the towers first appeared all manner of fantastic tales were told. Cars mysteriously came to a halt when passing Poling Corner and even a local farmer was heard to comment "Isn't there any danger of these death-rays getting out of control"!

(By kind permission of Mr. A. Oliver).

Below. To end with we have chosen a relic about which we are able to say very little. The source was a Bf109 that was shot down by Flying Officer Oxspring flying a No. 66 Squadron Spitfire from RAF Gravesend. The Germans were operating free lance fighter operations over the southeast when this 109 was engaged. Unable to escape the pilot, Lt. Bodendick, baled out and was captured. His plane, with no one at the controls, crashed at 5.05pm at Guilton Ash near Sandwich.

The site was subsequently excavated and a number of parts discovered. These included fragments of the engine, a complete tail wheel, cockpit instruments, an identity plate and even the control column. In amongst all these was this small relic. Despite much research its use remains unknown. What can be said is that it is probably an exterior fitting. It is a pale blue colour, and there are also the remains of a red arrow painted facing the buckle. Answers on a postcard please!

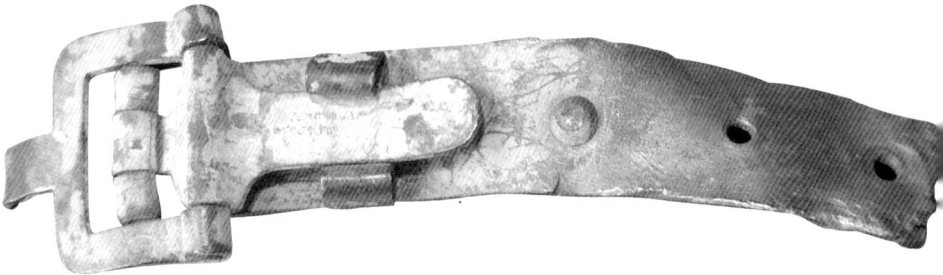

www.historicmilitarypress.com.